Wyatt Earp

Electric Book
Award Winner

Wyatt Earp

LARRY BECKETT

Alternating Current Press
Boulder, Colorado

Wyatt Earp
Larry Beckett

Alternating Current
Boulder, Colorado
alternatingcurrentarts.com

ISBN: 978-1-946580-17-7
First Edition: March 2020

ADVANCE PRAISE

"Whoever said that the long poem is dead, was dead wrong. Larry Beckett's elegant, hefty *Wyatt Earp* proves that the extended poetical narrative is alive and well and still kicking up its heels, spurs and all. Mining history, legend, and biography, Beckett has reinvented the American West and recreated one of its best-known gunfighters and lawmen, world-famous for his role during the deadly shootout at the O.K. Corral. Almost everyone who grew up watching *Gunsmoke*, *Have Gun—Will Travel*, and *Maverick* will enjoy Beckett's journey back in time. In *Wyatt Earp*, the landscapes feel authentic, the frontier towns seem as alive and dangerous as ever, and the voices of the Old West echo loudly and clearly. Beckett's poem is a hoot that provides real entertainment from beginning to end, and all the way through. If you have to get out of Dodge, or some other dusty town or derelict city, take Beckett's *Wyatt Earp* with you, and leave your six-guns at home."

—Jonah Raskin,
author of *American Scream: Allen Ginsberg's 'Howl' and the Making of the Beat Generation*

"Decades in the making with whiskey, gunsmoke, and trail dust enough to catch in your desert-parched throat, this whip-smart and vivid masterpiece breathes new and rarefied air into its re-envisioning of the Earp legend. Scattershot and peppered throughout with lines that crackle like a prairie wildfire, Beckett delivers both a Beat and gritty epic rich with spit-blood and ferocious poetic detail and a magnum opus few ever even dream of attempting. Honestly, you'd have to be a madman to try such a book—much less to pull it off—but Beckett is exactly the gunman for the job. A highwater mark and instant addition not only to his canon but to American poetry writ large."

—Hosho McCreesh,
author of *Chinese Gucci*

"From his beginnings in the 1960s writing lyrics, through his more recent down-to-earth academic-level explorations of the Beat Generation writers, to this new epic-length prose poem about Wild West icon Wyatt Earp, writer Larry Beckett has captured America in all of its manifestations—cultural, political, and historical. He and his writing are beautiful."

—Pat Thomas,
author of *Did It! Jerry Rubin: An American Revolutionary*
and producer of Allen Ginsberg's *The Last Word on First Blues*

"Larry Beckett's *Wyatt Earp* is a work for the ages, an American epic, vivid, alive, and utterly compelling. This heroic song of the West as prose poem unfolds with strength, vigor, and sovereign originality. Like the American "West" for whom its protagonist stands as metaphor, Beckett's *Wyatt* invents itself. In refreshing contrast to recent serious longform poetry, this anti-cow-boy saga succeeds without a whiff of meta-discourse, though that is abundantly available to the analytic reader. In *Earp,* Beckett has created that rare sustained poem whose primary material simply thrills. By substituting rhetorical devices for metric repetition, and by drawing out the sonorities and tonalities of Earp's distinctly western voice via notably de-punctuated dialogue, this Tombstone Homeric brings a remarkable new way of telling into the American tradition. Like Melville's potent incorporation of whalemen's speech into *Moby-Dick;* Whitman's long lines; William Carlos Williams' capture of the poetry inherent in Paterson's vernacular; Kerouac's steaming and streaming bop prosody; the taut telegraphic dialogue of film noir; and Tom Wolfe's *Kandy-Kolored Tangerine-Flake Streamline Baby,* Beckett's epic markedly expands the bound and prospect of the American tongue. If you want a poem that will take and ever change you, walk through Tombstone with *Wyatt Earp.*"

—Marc Zegans,
author of *La Commedia Sotterranea* and *The Book of Clouds*

The languages and landscapes that Larry Beckett captures in *Wyatt Earp* are intricately drawn and bitingly original. Here is a poet embracing that Brautigan beat attitude before taking us swiftly and deftly, as quickly as Earp's draw, off into the Sonoran Desert and into barrooms "after midnight, when the aces burn off, and the pharaoh rules in the down and out dynasties." This collection digs deep into character and style with wit and a deep understanding of Earp to reveal a world teetering off "in the distance between desire and consummation."

—Michael Garrigan,
author of *Robbing the Pillars*

"The poems in Larry Beckett's *Wyatt Earp* simmer and hiss, conjuring the sounds and imagery of the Old West. You can almost hear the rattle of a sidewinder and the jangly chime of spurs on outlaw boots walking the dirt streets of Tombstone, see tumbleweeds twisting in dusty wind and the flash of gunmetal under an unforgiving sun. This spectacular, historic collection is cinematic and wild, full of whiskey-drenched tavern tales and swaggering shootouts, all loaded like a gunslinger's pine box on an eerie, anachronistic ghost train of Beat poetry."

—V. C. McCabe,
author of *Give the Bard a Tetanus Shot*

FIVE ACTS

1

Arizona Territory 15
Tombstone 16
Mexican Quarter 17
Allen Street 18
Prayer for What Vanished 19
Sulphur Springs Valley 20
Soldiers Hole 21
Cosmopolitan Hotel 23
Law Office 25
Capital Saloon 27
Ballad of Mattie 28
Fort Griffin 29
Capital Saloon 33
Sixth and Allen 35

2

Tombstone, November 9, 1880 39
Wells, Fargo & Co. 40
Charleston 42
Oriental Building 43
Oriental Saloon 45
Wanted 46
San Pedro Road 47
Prayer to the Silence 49
Oriental Back Yard 50
Sixth Street 51
Mule Mountains 53
Allen Street 54
Alhambra Saloon 56
Fifth Street 58

3

Occidental Saloon 63
Allen Street 65
After Prayer 66
Mexican Quarter 67
Fly's Boarding House 68
Fifth Street 69

Recorder's Court 70
Fourth and Allen 72
Fourth and Allen 73
Fourth Street 75
Lumberyard 76
Fremont Street 78

4

Fremont Street 83
Prayer for the Dead 84
Sixth Street 85
Judge's Office 87
Judge's Office 89
Cosmopolitan Hotel 92
Fifth Street 95
Western Union Telegraph Company 96
Allen Street 97
Occidental Saloon 98
Tombstone, February 1, 1882 99
Fremont Street 101

5

Attorney's Office 105
Campbell and Hatch's Saloon 106
Benson Road 108
Mexican Quarter 109
Southern Pacific 111
Tucson Station 113
Cosmopolitan Hotel 114
South Pass 116
Unanswered Prayer 118
Iron Springs 119
Whetstone Mountains 121
Sulphur Springs Valley 123

Ballad of Mattie 125
Sources 127
About the Author 131
About the Cover 132
Colophon 133

Wyatt Earp

1

ARIZONA TERRITORY

Out over the snow-shot Chiricahuas, sideslipping on the sullen air, the sun, scorning the high pines, and the black oaks, the sharp junipers, wallowing to get wind of any dead flesh under the buckthorn on the lower slopes, green rattler, fox squirrel, body, warping its wings, shadows, hissing, is drifting down the pillars of cloud:

on the outskirts of the Sonoran desert, all of it keeps back what water it can from the sun, in secret, in the thorns of the mesquite, spines of the saguaro, cholla thicket, paloverde, ocotillo sticks, stalks of the manzanita, yucca, creosote, the yellow grass:

the sun, a bullet hole in the last west, the blue, bleeding orange, bleeding coral, is flooding the heavens as red as blood, as the buzzard's skin, and the dark, breaking, gives sanctuary to any, the outlaw hour, invisible.

In the distance, a couple of hoodlum wagons and a string of horses are dusting across the reaches of the San Pedro, on toward Goose Flats.

TOMBSTONE

Wyatt Earp rides in, night without stars, Tombstone, dismounts in Dodge City, trail's end, in the buffalo grass, dust blowing in his face, loops his black racehorse to the hitching rail, Everything goes in Wichita, cow-boys leaning outside, and goes into the Grand Hotel, the kerosene light, the tack piano doing *The Blue Tail Fly.* He gets this medicine: shack for now around the corner from that new O.K. Corral; south of the Dead Line, the Santa Fe tracks, is all honkytonks and hells, to the river; across the toll bridge, dance halls, sideshows, and Dixie Lee's bordello; no call for a stage line, mail and express already going; try the Oriental and deal in pasteboard and ivory; Texas boys might hurrah the town, pilgrim, the mayor would like a peace officer; no city hall, courthouse, jail; but robbery in daylight, whores in gingham; silver miners, whip cracking in the street, to start the nude saloon girl race: dust is a citizen, and the stars don't matter. He slips outside, and his long horse is gone.

theys only one Wyatt Earp story his book of *Genesis* told over in a power of ways now Virg in 61 you was off in the Union infantry out in Tennessee and us little brothers back in Iowa and Wyatt just 13 ah Morg he says I hate looking at that mules tail and this turning the grass upside down 80 acres all corn and hes hearing the bugle and one day runs away half days ride to Ottumwa and the recruiting office and wouldnt you know daddy is there and hauls him back he gets the switch ands fixing to give him a hiding and mama says Nick laying her hand on his shoulder he done nothing wrong and daddys arm jolts her out of the way and Wyatt so steady so brave steps in between and eye to eye You cant hit mama and daddy drops the switch

ALLEN STREET

The fire always breaks out in the Arcade Saloon, some damn fool lighting a cigar by the whiskey barrel blowing out the door into Allen Street, and the stores catching, the clothing burning, and the dry goods, the Oriental burning, the Lion burning, the Magnolia Saloon, the dance house burning, the bankrolls burning, the sun at 100 degrees, the district court burning, the judge's office burning, and the undertaker's, the Eagle burning, the Alhambra burning, Fifth Street burning west, east, burning north, south, the Occidental burning, the Cosmopolitan, Wyatt Earp walking through the smoke with a Winchester in his arms and seeing a woman on a balcony, Hafford's Saloon burning, Brown's Hotel burning, and the gun store, bullets banging, letters burning, the newspaper burning, and the Tivoli Saloon, the Grand Hotel burning, the hoisting works whistle, the hook and ladder, Tombstone is burning. At dusk, the mayor comes back from the east with a fire engine and two hose carriages.

PRAYER FOR WHAT VANISHED

That trail, not cold,
into the back country,
the sign, old music,
or the scent, tallgrass,
to Illinois, the garden,
before the flood
and the outlaws,
ah god, those fields,
at morning, green,
unknown: the hills,
the creeks, downpouring:
Urilla's kiss: that thrill:
out of the Mississippi: sparrows:
the prairies: that peace.

SULPHUR SPRINGS VALLEY

Oh I am a Texas cow-boy The rangers, in a battalion, drove them like longhorns, out of the Lone Star. Into this territory. So easy to make them out: none of them in a John B., white shirt, black coat, like a citizen; they're all *just off the stormy plains* slicked up, with a big sombrero the color of dust, red bandanna at the neck, wool shirt, doeskin trousers, half boots. *My trade is cinchin saddles* They fight off Apaches, go down Sonora way, *and pullin bridle reins* steal cattle and keep them at the Clanton ranches in San Pedro and the Animas, at the McLaurys in Sulphur Springs, sell beef cheap, pay dollars, drink. *Oh I can tip a lariat* They like to shoot peace officers *with the greatest of ease*, think it's in the name of the lost cause. Few arrested, less tried, none convicted. Curley Bill can whirl his pistol *I can rope a streak o lightnin* and cock it as it rises *ride any damn where I please.*

SOLDIERS HOLE

rain threatening
you Frank McLaury
in the door of the twisting house and the corral empty
this is my layout off limits to you and your platoon
word is Curley Bill rustled six mules out of the camp and fencing them is a federal crime this is US Deputy Marshal Virgil Earp
who are them civilians youre violating my rights
his specials Morgan and what you got there Wyatt
its the iron D8
it blots the US brand just right eh Frank
dont go looking for em lieutenant I cant answer for my brother and the boys here theyll start shooting
well
Im known in the Territory never been called a thief youre here to protect me you coward bring all this posse down on me maybe you stole and sold em Ill let Arizona decide
easy Frank return them and well drop the charges
till manana in Charleston a word with you star men
under his breath
what business is it of yours if a few government hard tails go missing the folks round here dont care if they get em cheap and dont love the army anyway the sheriff dont care and as for gunshy the fools on him
how come
I aint bringing no mules back and one more thing
you ever follow us up this close well kill you
look for me Im Wyatt Earp and tomorrow Im

wiring Tucson and accepting as deputy its not you
not I its the law break it and I will ride into your
dust
first drops

COSMOPOLITAN HOTEL

Im only saying youre tending bar here
yeah
anyone can see youre Buckskin Frank
oh yeah
from your getup
yeah
youre gallivanting with this chambermaid
yeah May
whos married to that bartender
yeah but they split
I see trouble
well youre on the inside he told me if her and you go to the ball coming with the quadrille band
Ill shoot you
or one of his pals
yeah
I know youre a dead shot
yeah
anything can happen
thanks for the warning
yeah
hey I hear you got brothers going against you in Sulphur Springs
I got my own brothers to go against them
oh yeah
like that time in Missouri the hell with it
what happened Wyatt
hard to
never get over it till you do
on the outskirts of town I was constable and my bride Urilla her brothers and one you knocked her up and killed her and I it aint so it was the yellow fever and no amount of quinine she burned and he if youre not too yellow take off

your gun Im giving you the beating of your life before I run you out of here and I where you want to do this and he this lot I hand my badge and Colt to my brother and he when I rough and tumble you that pains for the pain you give us and I dont talk so much lets get this over he springs at me and I sidestep and bang his jaw and hes off balance and drops in the dust gets up comes on I slam him in the belly he doubles I upper cut him on the chin and hes out and I anybody else want any and my brothers looking at them
ever lose a fight Wyatt
never

(reading)

The Clerk: Mr Leslie, also known as Buckskin Frank, in the victim's own saloon, Lowry and Archer's, was telling the accused that a citizen handed Wyatt Earp a wire saying deliver the prisoner for the shooting at the Headquarters Saloon to him, and the deputy sheriff said the sheriff can spell his own name, this is a forgery, when the victim's wife invited the said Buckskin Frank next door to the Cosmopolitan Hotel, to whisper with him on the dark porch, and in his dying statement, the victim said he saw the two and was going when the accused said Look out Frank here is Mike, and both opened fire, the victim wrestled with them and was shot, and though Buckskin Frank was arrested by Wyatt Earp, the judge ruled out the dying statement and set him at liberty, when the accused was arrested by Wyatt Earp.

Mr Jones: Your honor, in light of the fact that you were Buckskin Frank's counsel in the foregoing case and justice of the peace at his wedding, I would ask that in this case against the friend he was covering for when he confessed to the shooting, that you recuse yourself.

The Court: Who are you to question my integrity? As I'm newly appointed? I order you to apologize, and to quit this courtroom.

(pointing to door)

Mr Jones: I will not apologize; I have a constitutional right to be in this courtroom.

The Court: I cite you for contempt. Deputy, arrest the counsel for the defense.

(the deputy sheriff does not obey)

The Court: You damn

(the judge jumps up and collars the counsel for the defense)

Mr Jones: What the

(the counsel for the defense flails and slaps the judge)

The Court: How dare

(the deputy sheriff parts them, and they resume their chairs)

The Court: I fine you twenty-five dollars for contempt and sentence you to a day in the county jail for striking a justice of the peace. Deputy, escort him to jail.

Mr Earp: You can walk around; I'll meet you at the stage depot.

The Court: What? I order you to arrest the counsel and you stand there like a flagpole. I order you to escort him to jail and you let him walk. You will appear in these chambers tomorrow as I cite you for contempt.

Mr Earp: Your honor, as soon as you adjourn this court, you're under arrest, for assault.

CAPITAL SALOON

its the way of gunfighting first heard it from my daddy in a wagon train going west through the cornhuskers out here your life at any moment might hang on if youre ready to fight for it these western camps are free and easy and you might stretch a point and let a man off but when youre up against pure vicious thats our old enemy and when that outlaw forces it you go as far as you have to hit first and hit to kill and in that legendary summer Kansas City in Market Square on the bench in front of the police station talking buffalo hunting with those old scouts Cheyenne Jack Old Man Keeler Wild Bill Hickok that hard winter bunch making history it turns to gunplay and Jack Gallagher Boot Hill is full of them who pulled the trigger before aiming and got a halo for nothing they can quickdraw and fill both hands or one fanning or shoot from the hip no chance against you if you slack off and pull the trigger once and next season on the plains out on the Salt Fork its Bat Masterson no tricks no show no bluff no hurry and let your muscles think faster than thinking first shot last shot and tells me how its courage that stands you up to them and nerve keeps you cool only way to quickdraw is to take your time Ive never had to use this wisdom but I got to be a crack shot the gun just above my waist Id fire five shots from one hand the border shift to the other five shots at a hundred yards into the capital O of Office by the time I and I met Mattie on the way time I met you Doc in that Texas water hole three years gone

BALLAD OF MATTIE

Off of the farm,
on to the lights,
that sixteen runaway's
in his sights.

He's on the trail of this outlaw
out of Dodge, east to Fort Scott:
in a parlor house, girl of the night,
and he was caught.

With her shadow hair
and her shy way,
she let him in:
he lost a day.

He's on the trail of this outlaw
but she was dear when she was bought:
the stars laid out the common law,
and he was caught.

FORT GRIFFIN

on the flats by the Clear Fork this bare saloon
pardon me
the backbar black cherry with scrolls of gilt the mirror the nude and the dog asking
on the trail long
I been reading sign through the Nations on down the Brazos
whatll it be sir
what it was only I wish youd won that day in Cheyenne in 68
for the love of christ is it yourself behind that moustache Wyatt Earp
hey Shannsey imagine you
he knocked me out of prizefighting altogether so he did
well thats no
its nothing I do be thinking of look at you jesus youre a man
Id take a schooner of
ah youre the saint that wont touch whoopee water only one in all the railroad camps you want mineral
thats right
there you go now
what do I
on the house hold on heres to stealing lying fighting cheating and drinking may you steal kisses lie in her arms fight for your brother cheat death drink in the wonder
remember that
what is it sign you say what brings you down into the panhandle
Im after Dirty Dave
for the bounty

for this holdup on a Santa Fe train him and Roarke hightailed it know where he mightve gone
from here across the Staked Plains or towards the Rio Grande sure I dont know
its a long shot
but that man there would
nodding at him whispers
Doc Holliday
in a pearl suit ash hair blue-eyed and haggard at solitaire
know him
hes the killer isnt he I dont figure him friendly to a peace officer
I hear hes killed but nobody round here
nodding to the old bareknuckle fighter and stepping to the window
morning Mister Holliday the bar-tender tipped me to you Im Wyatt Earp
eye to eye
call me
hacking
call me
curling over his chest his hand out to shake no palm up wait till the coughing
call me Doc everyone does absolute misnomer
strong steady grip
for some reason they dont want me leaning over them while they open wide
Wyatt smiling
only gentlemen in this sanctuary are scouts soldiers muleskinners bullwhackers sage rats cold deck cardplayers trail hands cattle rustlers horse

thieves land sharps which are you
bounty hunter
well if you will allow me to finish this round of ace in the hole Ill surrender without a
Wyatt laughing
struggle
Im looking for Dirty Dave
for the bounty
pouring a tall whiskey knocking it back
he hit a pay train Im only trying to get those boys their dollars
out here as the bard says in a wildernesse where are no lawes
what wayd he go
give me a day and Ill get his trail for you out for justice eh well Ill take the bounty for my trouble
his slender fingers turning the cards
aint seen the like of that smoke pole in your cross draw holster
shining nickel barrel ivory grips
Colt Lightning
they say he showed you to draw and shoot and you showed him to draw to a pair of aces
its a legend Id have nothing to do with that sidewinder
hes tough that Arkansas rancher the grass is waving over him and he done it
nothing to me been carving credits on my gun barrel since I shot that saloon keeper in Dallas had to move on that soldier hand of freeze out in Jacksboro move on stabbed a tinhorn in Denver move on wounded a sport in Trinidad how many have I downed

ever arrested
why no I happen to I
happen to what
youre a true heart Wyatt never thought Id and I cant throw dust at you its all words words I make up dime novels as I go old Deadwood shooting my way on and the bad hombres they keep their distance
never arrested
once for quote playing at a game of cards in a house in which spirituous liquors are sold
thanks for levelling Doc
till tomorrow sir

CAPITAL SALOON

it was the Missus here whos my salvation down
in Texas after I told you Fort Davis
I trailed him there and on to Fort Clark Fort
Concho Fort McKavett back to Fort Griffin and I
got word from Dodge he doubled back into Kan-
sas hit another train for ten thousand was caught
heading south by Bat Masterson and a posse and
I got wind of you
about the
they said you killed a man
how generous of them Im playing blind with this
tinhorn whos monkeying with the deadwood and
I warn him play poker say it again at last I pull
down the sugar without showing my hand
perfect right
he pulls his six gun and I operate on his ribs with
a penknife
dont your conscience get you
I coughed it up long ago
youre under arrest
in the hotel lobby thinking his associates are go-
ing to lynch me sure though hes only bleeding
swallowing her whiskey and catching her breath
I hear those miners hollering and look in a back
window till I see Doc
Im meditating on the brevity of our days when I
hear Fire
I get this other six shooter and mine and tether
this horse in the alley burn a shed bang on the
hotel Fire they all run out and I slip in cover the
deputy with one gun and toss the other laughing
Come on Doc
and youre a dance hall girl
we hide in the willows get Docs plunder and

horses and drag it for Dodge
ah Dodge my dear the gateway to the what is that
story the conductor to a rough on the train
ticket
aint got no ticket
where you going
going to hell
thatll be one dollar you get off at Dodge
you asked and angled for everything about that
cowtown
did I
are there saloons where I can work start at the
Long Branch you still assistant city marshal so I
can cover you in a scrape with the law you really
a deacon yes at the First Union Church is there
a hotel where I can luxury the Dodge House
dont matter where he holes up his hearts down
in Georgia all them billets doux
one too many whiskeys dont ruin it honey
whats her name Doc she your cousin
why I call you Big Nose Kate
hes in your whirl Wyatt let him go
I go where I please queen of the alley
Im going to Globe the hell with you
I wont forget you shell be back

SIXTH AND ALLEN

After midnight, when the aces burn off, and the pharaoh rules in the down and out dynasties, this player was coppering his card to lose in the Bank Exchange Saloon, when shots, outside, ah it must be cow-boys shooting the moon out of the sky. Wyatt Earp, dealing, off duty, unarmed, steps into the street, the McLaury brothers, guns out, flash, running toward the fire, Morgan, behind a chimney, and who is it, Dodge, give me your gun, sudden bullets off of the bricks, comes out of cover, across from the whores' cribs and cabins, I am an officer, Marshal White's voice, give me your pistol, gets in behind, it's Curley Bill, who draws it, White's hand on the barrel, Wyatt's arms around his chest, and White, now you son of a bitch give up that pistol, jerks it, it fires, I am shot, Wyatt buffaloes the shooter, squatting over White, they're sniping at him, to his brother, put out the fire his coat is burning, to Curley Bill, get up, and hauls him by the shirt, what have I done I done nothing it went off at half cock you cant arrest me:

what have you done you yellow god damn dog you gut shot the law and I know it hell die theyll close up gambling for a day the preacher will drawl on the great unknown and a thousand will follow his wound up to Boot Hill the vigilantes will come to string you up Ill stand them off and at your murder trial cause I didnt see you trigger him my testimony will let you go free but you best look over your shoulder among the willows Im coming Im an angel flying through the badlands and Ill keep on till you atone for this that silence is heaven all music my trumpet the thunder my voice and the requital your last breath

2

TOMBSTONE, NOVEMBER 9, 1880

Charles Shibell, Pima County Sheriff
San Xavier Hotel
Tucson

Dear Sir,

I have the honor herewith to resign the office of deputy sheriff of Pima County.

The election of one week past was rigged, and you won by fraud, committed by the cow-boys. The voting inspector was Ike Clanton, who has been stealing cattle from Texas John. The precinct judge was Johnny Ringo, who is a killer from the Hoodoo war on the innocent. The San Simon polling place was Joe Hill's cabin, who is a rustler. From there, Curley Bill, who shot our marshal, rode into Tombstone that morning with the crooked votes that tipped it to you. He may hang for murder, and is relying on my testimony; he has agreed to confess this fraud.

I know you'll choose Johnny Behan to replace me; he is a glad hand man, not a peace officer, and is looking forward to joining your tax-skimming 10 Percent Ring. I will get a recount and overturn this election, clear to the Supreme Court. But I cannot go on as your deputy.

Respectfully,
Wyatt S. Earp

WELLS, FARGO & CO.

Wyatt Earp, waiting to ride shotgun messenger on the next stage to the Southern Pacific, looks out and here's Virg, raging in on a buckboard, thought he was riding south to the Last Chance claim, who's that in manacles, Johnny Behind-the-Deuce, that quiet faro crack always playing the two spot open to buck the bank, shivering it was self defense, they're flying from a lynch mob. He sends Virg for help, and lays a scatter gun in the crook of his arm, crossing to the skinny door of Vogan's Bowling Alley and Saloon, where he surrounds Johnny with his brothers, Doc, and four men, and leads them over to the livery stable.
stand back open passage Im taking this man to the Tucson jail
the law is failing and you know he wont stand trial were hanging him
stand back: it minds him of that time in Dodge City, where he invented buffaloing, don't shoot to kill like Wild Bill, and wound the boulevards, but grab their gun hand and crack their skull with the barrel of the Peacemaker, when the cow-hands, flinging shots into the Comique Theater, at the marshal, and he and Jim Masterson fire back into the night, toward the toll bridge, and this kid falls, and this night, in front of the Long Branch, they get the drop on him, start shooting, and Doc in there at faro with Cockeyed Frank slams out with a pistol and a six gun and wings the leader in the shoulder so Wyatt can draw and buffalo him:
throw em up all the way and empty
throw em up: it minds him of that time in Wich-ita, when all the bosses, all the hands, out of

Rowdy Joe's and Red Beard's, out of the saloons and whorehouses across the river come riding in a mob to the bridge to pay Wichita back for when he and four men going to repossess that bad debt piano from the madam, he says to them you're too cheap to help her out, if you take my advice you'll never go into anything you can't buy out of, and he leads his officers and citizens to the bridge, spread out and hard to shoot, all six shooters drawn, all hell about to break.
He keeps on looking at the gun man:
put away your guns mind me now Mannen put up that gun and go on home
Clements puts his pistol into his holster and turns his horse. And they all go back to the dives and deadfalls.
He keeps on looking at the cattle king:
you Tobe youre next
Driskill puts his pistol into his holster and turns his back. And he motions them all toward the calaboose.
He keeps on looking at the mine operator:
nice mob didnt know you trailed with such company Dick dont be a fool back off any of you attack this posse Dick here gets it
Gird puts his pistol into his holster and turns on his heel. And he leads Johnny Behind-the-Deuce into the stable. They could a got me easy, but no one fired a shot.

CHARLESTON

where you been Doc
water rights claims in the Huachacas
Scar Face was right thats my long horse
whose corral is it
its the road agent that Johnny Behan made deputy here Frank Stilwell
lovely it makes robbing stages so much less trouble if youre wearing a star
its the Clantons
theyre going to take it out Wyatt
all right Im going to keep it peaceful with that fire breathing man hey Ike
what do you want
well theres a subpoena for you on this election fraud and Sheriff Behans coming with a posse to arrest you and haul you to Tucson
yeah if he finds us Im arming everyone I wont stand it
he slips around the corner
a posse
I was bluffing
Billy you cant take that horse out its mine and Ive got papers from Tombstone that
take it got any more horses to lose
Ill stable them so you wont have a chance to steal them
he drops a rope as reins over the horse

ORIENTAL BUILDING

were nearer to the stars of heaven up here
I like the roof because it catches air
hey Wyatt you seen that dancer I was shotgun on the stage that brung her in with the opera from the Golden Gate
no I aint is
all curves and Bat says shes the belle of the honky tonks
that right
living with Johnny of all people
all politics why Governor Fremont made him sheriff of the new county and this days after the cow-boys shot up the Alhambra Saloon
that Curley Bill
yes and the fourflusher broke his promise to make me undersheriff
he say why
he didnt like that bluff I pulled on Ike
out at Charleston
yes and I hit his faro table one night and broke his god damn bank Ill take mine in cash your credit dont cover a white chip
her name is Josephine something
I bet hes cheating on her now
I tell you because you and Mattie
I know Morg Im drifting away I dont know how
hey Wyatt I been reading in the gospel
that right
that part where it says To day shalt thou be with me in paradise
I remember
where do you think we go after
where are the snows I saw falling on Illinois
just gone

aint no other place
I wonder
no inferno no glory
but how is there justice
in our hands here
maybe the body fails and the soul flies
ah this world is gunsmoke curling into the void
if youre right well never know
only one thing lasts
whats that
history

ORIENTAL SALOON

In through the wings, Wyatt Earp, in the long saloon, as she slides by, first sight, her fingers this hour, her bosom love, her eyes adventure, asks the iceman, after, she don't go by Josephine, left just before, come back right after, and he's on her trail, his law, desire. He looks up and down, his heart beginning, and Bat Masterson shows him where at the bar she lifted up a gin fizz. He guesses she'll stay away from the faro table, and circles to cross by the silver mirror, cut over to the nude, on down the line. Daylight, and he's on his way, by the dark bottles; two days across the sawdust, toward the cash register, when a hard rain wipes out all signs of her. That night, by the upright piano, he hears from a dancing girl, that dancer, here not long ago, and in a rush. He picks up a trace east, and loses it next day, overtaken by rain. He makes for a table lolling at the back, and knows her by her legs, the way she moves. I'm Wyatt Earp. It's a pleasure to happen on you. May I call you Sadie?

WANTED

The beauty
of the hurdy-gurdies
Josephine
Sarah
Marcus
alias Sadie
also known as
May Bell
dancing in the Pinafore
as the captain's daughter
Josephine

For sliding by me
in the saloon

With her opera eyes
with her Cochise County tears
with her lover
that liar
in bed with married
with her manifest breasts
with her slim destiny
with her curves
in this flatland
with her fingers now
I'd love to lace
with her voice like water
in the future
with her by-and-by
like a memory kiss

Reward:
all the heart I have

SAN PEDRO ROAD

man in the brush by the river
you got him Morg
yeah
Wyatt lighting
you Luther King
yes I
you jumped out of that corral what you running
for
thought you was outlaws
were trailing outlaws
I was going to milk the cow
with two revolvers in your belt
well I
and two winded horses tethered
was going to
know anything about the Benson stage holdup
nothing
you leave that cow pony at Wheatons old barn
no I
I seen you riding it last week in Tombstone
I aint been there in a fortnight
all right Johnny its the Redfields Im going to look
around dont let him talk to them
he walks to the shack looks over his shoulder
thought I said dont let them talk god damn it now
Redfields going to tip off the rest
I dont take orders from you
Luther come down here
around the barn out of sight of the sheriff
youre up Salt Creek aint you you dont know nothing well I been after you cow-boys and I know youre in that deserted adobe on Contention Road reading Deadwood Dicks Last Act cause you tore out the end is that it in your pocket the stage

goes by with a shotgun and that means bullion as they slow on a grade three men bandannas over their faces come out of the chaparral with rifles saying hold up and when my old friend Bud cracks the whip hes shot through the heart and his woman and kids in Calistoga are cut loose youre firing on the stage and the man outside looks at the moon last time now the sheriff says the trails twelve hours old and hopeless and I say I can pick up the sign I follow you to the Dragoon hills to Tres Alamos you doubling your tracks and riding in the riverbed and on living rock and clouding your trail to Wheatons lost ranch I find you here you long riders are all in the Clantons outfit Leonard Head Crane and you well the man who watched the horses is lucky he wont swing for the double murder

thats me I held the horses it was them shooting

Johnny are you hearing this and youre at Redfields ranch

for ammo and money to bring to our camp

and where is that

I wont run him in on suspicion and you have no authority Wyatt

the stage was carrying mail Ill arrest him on a federal warrant

they ride on into the desolation

PRAYER TO THE SILENCE

The shooting star
at the toll bridge
that night in Dodge:
let it not be my bullet
in his back: and I,
Why shoot at me,
is there a thousand
dollar bounty
by the cattle men,
because I locked up
their boss? and he,
stars in his eyes:
That last roundup,
a thousand head.

ORIENTAL BACK YARD

you loudmouthed to him
Ike in motion Wyatt standing
I told him nothing
well he knows everything
what did he say
am I dealing with you
to surrender Leonard
yeah if the cow-boys
and the mans ranch
down on the border
he know you jumped it
you said no strings
all I wants glory and the election
for the dollars as sheriff
to end the cow-boys
you talk Im dead
why would I betray you
you pulled that bluff
out at Charleston
subpoena on me
trying to keep it peaceful
why is Williams
look you want the reward
cause he wont be taken
dead or alive I had him
without a fight
telegraph Wells Fargo
well whys he pumping me
hes shooting at the moon
what for
is he drinking
Ike motionless Wyatt walking away

SIXTH STREET

I thank you sir for my liberty what was the bail 5 grand cash only ah well at least its not that fell arrest with out all bayle as the bard says but what kind of institution is this to which I was remanded jailhouse is too fine a word for it nothing more than an abandoned cathouse my lord the squalor to which I Doc Holliday southern gentleman and upright gambler was reduced I don't mean to trouble you Wyatt say the word and Ill leave Tombstone but not before telling you how I was arrested for the Benson stage murders King whom you caught well Johnny saw to it he wasnt confined in this calaboose but in a flophouse on the outskirts and miracles do exist in the night he managed to take the deputys guns and ammunition go out the back way to a waiting horse and ride for old Mexico now that the guilty were free it was time to frame the innocent there had been if you read it articles in that cow-boy rag attempting to diminish the splendor of my reputation by accusing me of this holdup I imagine because Im the only one of your allies with a shadow though it was my invention and its you they want to end the rumors were waning when I had lets call it a contretemps with Big Nose Kate in which I may have referred to her in less than loving terms that is as a hag a red light sister a pig a slut an idiot a hussy a tart a harlot a strumpet and an outright whore she did not take this with the best grace but looked for solace in a bottle of whiskey and after swore out an affidavit for Johnny implicating yours truly in the crime now that afternoon I was in fact at Leonards shack at The Wells old business friend from New Mexico have you heard him read Wild Bills story out loud I returned with the water and Old Man Fuller on the Charleston road and everybody at the faro table that evening can alibi me including you besides if it was me Id a downed the horse and come away with the gold unlike these desperadoes shooting two men for nothing whats that send her away Ill satisfy you I have a roll in the Oriental safe Ill peel off a thousand and shell depart for Globe singing Love oh Love oh careless Love

MULE MOUNTAINS

In the firs and manzanita, on the bad road, in the shivering rain, the night before, the driver said, the Bisbee stage, carrying the Copper Queen payroll, was stopped, men in bandannas, one with a shotgun, one with a Colt, men in the chaparral, and saying hold on, taking the gold-mount ivory-handle six guns from the Wells, Fargo man, and saying, give up the sugar, everyone knows that's deputy Frank Stilwell's word for money when he's in a game, and he saw through the mask to Pete Spence, his summer name, who is Lark Ferguson, the Texas killer, and the locals said them and Curley Bill and Pony Deal, come back from the Skeleton Canyon massacre, had been all afternoon in the Blind Trail saloon. In the mud this morning, Wyatt Earp is looking at the nailheads in the bootprint, and, with his brother Morg, slopes down into Bisbee, where he sights new bootheels on the deputy going into the saloon, and turns up the old, with the nailheads, at the bootmaker's, invoice to Stilwell, who says you can arrest me, round up Spence, but our confederates will lie us elsewhere in the face of the judge, and it won't stick.

ALLEN STREET

late afternoon
almighty god Wyatt they was in black robes black masks and kissed the six shooter to join the secret Citizens Safety mob
in masks theyre outlaws Virg
its twice as hard
secret hell theyre in the papers
to keep the peace theyre sick of our bad sheriff and no convictions
who isnt hey look by the Alhambra is that Morg inside that circle
they see Ike Clanton Billy Clanton Frank McLaury Tom McLaury Joe Hill Milt Hicks Johnny Ringo
Im town marshal and you know my deputy Frank you can tell us what youre saying
all right I tell you what you might arrest Stilwell and Spence but dont think you can arrest me you ever lay hands on me or my brother Ill down you all and Doc Holliday
if we have to come after you well get you
Morg walking away
why are you so riled aint just that holdup
I know youre getting up a vigilante committee to hang us
hang who
all us cow-boys
ah Frank you recollect when Curley Bill shot Marshal White who stood off the vigilantes
you did
who saved Johnny Behind-the-Deuce from being lynched
you did
you still believe were in this committee

I believe the man that told me
whos that
its the sheriff
you know Virg he hates me for stealing her love
I tell you it makes no difference what I do Ill never surrender my arms to you Id rather die fighting than get strangled
youre loco
one last thing Ringo
yeah Wyatt
we know all about your secret get together last spring and the cow-boys taking an oath over your blood to kill the Earp brothers we caught the stink from here
first stars

ALHAMBRA SALOON

Jack o diamonds jack o diamonds
is a hard card to play
I cant live one hour in this country if they discover it
I dont see how he could spread it around Ike as hes in Tucson ten days
you talk everything with him
here he is on the six o clock stage Doc I ever tell you Ike and I were in any deal
I was in the money Wyatt you dragged me out of the Fair for this no you never said a thing
Ike says I did
Ikes a goddamn liar
Im a dead man
what deal is that Ike
I give up your pal Leonard
for the reward
dead or alive
cow-boy selling out a cow-boy ever hear of loyalty
you double crosser you traitor you rounder you squealer you turntail you lowlife you villain you fraud you degenerate youre the original sidewinder
Im going to kill you
get your gun out and go to work
I got no gun
go heel yourself
tell you what
Ike walking to the Grand Hotel
Doc to the Oriental
next man puts me and Wyatt Earp in the same sentence Ill shoot him down
whats he up in arms about
evening Virg that madman just spilled to Doc the

deal he didnt want me to let on to him
well its hell outside on Allen Street with Curley Bill Stilwell Spence Johnny Ringo and all parading and saying theyre running the Earp brothers out of Tombstone in the next two days
in a showdown
looks like it Wyatt the vigilantes say theyll back us against them
I say no to that move itd bring on a free for all in the street
they deputized you Wyatt and you Morg and Doc and say its our call
well wait the Clantons and McLaurys are back of this show Ike just left for Sulphur Springs and we aint seen the rest in three four days theyll get nervous when nothing happens and come in the longer we keep them waiting the tougher it is for them
Virgil walking to the Occidental
Wyatt to the Eagle Brewery
I played the jack against the ace
and heaven looked me in the face

FIFTH STREET

Wyatt Earp
what is it now Ike
will you walk with me
what for
what for to talk with me
I cant go too far
whys that
I got to close the game
back there
back at the Brewery
you tell Doc Holliday no man
no man what
can talk to me that way and live
dont tangle with him
when Doc mocked me
just now
I wasnt fixed right
how so
no gun but in the morning
look Ike
Ill have him man to man
he dont want to fight
its been talk so long
long time
time to fetch it to a close
I wont fight no one
you wont
not if I can get away
how come
no money in it
in the morning
look Ike
Ill be ready for all of you
go sleep it off Ike

tomorrow
you talk too much for a fighting man
Ike going into the Brewery
the stars
Doc wavering on the street
out tonight
Ill walk you back
is the moon
you keep away from Clanton
all right
dont want a gunfight
keep away
with you in it
they go up Third Street to Fly's Boarding House
by the O.K. Corral

3

OCCIDENTAL SALOON

last hand its cockcrow
who chooses
the bucks to you Virg
five card draw high
anything wild
deuces Morg
you done shuffling
there
whorehouse cut Tom
all right deal
ante up Johnny
Im breathing
no bet
the actions on you Ike
five ivories
I see your five
Im in
I raise you five
pure bluff I cover it
to ten
all in I fold
dead money
Im in
Ill stand
with a made hand
three cards
hit me for two
and Ill draw one
I pass
I call your ten
I check
the showdown
three queens
tens up

the hell with you
ace full boys
another pot
its the break

ALLEN STREET

hold on Virg
whats that
I know you stand in with them
with who
who tried to murder me last night
who tried to
if so Im in town
I dont know what youre
and I got a message for Doc
whats that Ike
the damn bastard has got to fight
I see you armed Ill arrest you
no man can talk
dont want to hear you
to me that way
talking like that
tell him
now Im going down home
Im in the street
going to bed
sleep nothing off
I dont want you breaking the peace
you wont carry the message
hell no
Ike swinging away hand under his coat on his six
gun

AFTER PRAYER

I got a hold
of this trout, but
it wags away,
I see the water
is railroad tracks,
open boxcar,
in my hands, silver
scales, and this
man behind me's
firing a gun.
Who are you, sir?
I'm Independence
Day, deputy;
damn it, get up!

MEXICAN QUARTER

get up Wyatt hurry and get your clothes on I was done with my shift at the Oriental and I seen Ikes pistol in his belt I covered it with his coat and told him go to bed and he said no ah no when the Earps and Doc Holliday show on the street the ball will open this was by the telegraph office wire who Curley Bill or Johnny Ringo I dont know I know he said theyll have to fight youre what going back to bed all right theres likely to be hell

FLY'S BOARDING HOUSE

wake up Doc
what
are you still drunk
what time
Mary says Ikes downstairs
yeah what does Jesus say
waving a rifle
what time is it Kate
noon
so what
hes looking for you
if God will let me live long enough to get my clothes on he shall see me
buckling on his Colt Lightning

FIFTH STREET

Wyatt Earp, in a flat black sombrero, white shirt, in a long coat against the October wind, with his American Colt revolver on his hip, walks across patches of snow, into the Oriental Saloon. The attorney who wouldn't quit the courtroom is asking Virg. What does all this mean. What do you mean. Ike's out there armed with a Winchester and a Colt. Hunting you boys. Wyatt steps in. What happened to thou shalt not kill. Well, deacon, it's Tombstone. I'll go down, find him, see what he wants. Wyatt takes Allen Street, Virg and Morg take Fremont, and he walks by the brewery, the unfinished church, by the general store. Virg comes up behind Ike, grips the rifle by the barrel, Ike pulls his revolver out of his belt and as he turns to shoot Virg buffaloes him to the wooden sidewalk. You looking for us? I'd seen you a second before I'd a killed you. You're under arrest. Firearms inside the city limits.

RECORDER'S COURT

Ike bandannas his wound
Virg go for the judge
yeah Wyatt
okay you goddamn dirty cowthief you said youd assassinate me six times that I know Id be in my rights shooting you down anywhere I saw you
if you were a second later theyd be a coroners inquest seven
if you want to fight Ill go anywhere on earth Ill go over to the San Simon in your own crowd
fight is my racket all I wants four feet of ground and my six shooter
Morg holding his guns
Ill pay your fine if youll fight
Ill fight you anywhere anyway if I had a six shooter Id make a fight with you all
here if you want to make a fight so bad Ill give you mine
offering his Peacemaker Colt revolver
I dont like the odds
sit down
I fine you twenty-five dollars and two fifty court costs
where should I leave your guns
anywhere I can get them
outside the courthouse Wyatt comes up against Tom with his dead eyes
what are you doing here
nothing out for a stroll on Fremont Street
youre lying you're here on account of Ike
Im looking after him
you think you can menace us and abolish justice
I dont know what

are you heeled
you want a fight Ill fight you anywhere
all right right here jerk your gun and use it
he swings his hand Wyatt slaps him buffaloes
him blood branching down his face

FOURTH AND ALLEN

Wyatt Earp walks out of Hafford's Saloon, lighting a cigar. Frank McLaury and Billy Clanton, after drinks, swing out of the Grand Hotel, onto their horses, in their show-off rags, flat hats, wild shirts, high boots. Doc Holliday, by the Cosmopolitan, salutes them: How are you this fine day. They glare at him, turn up Fourth, dismount, go in Spangenberg's Pioneer Gun & Locksmith Shop, where Tom McLaury's sticking cartridges in his belt. Frank's bangtail steps up on the sidewalk, against the law; Wyatt strolls over and yanks it back into the street. The cow-boys shock, Billy lays his hand down on his pistol, Frank kicks out, snatches the reins, leads the horse away, as Ike walks up. Inside, the clerk looks at the wound on Ike's skull, and shakes his head. The cow-boys, in bright bandannas, loading their guns, stare out at Wyatt. Virg comes out of Wells, Fargo with a Stevens ten gauge shotgun.

FOURTH AND ALLEN

you the marshal
yeah who are you
I just blew in
what can I do
I seen
for you
I seen four five men wearing guns down by the O.K. Corral all salty and saying the troubles with you and theyre going to kill you kill all the Earps kill them on sight
thanks for the warning
what kind of town
afternoon Johnny
is this
whats the ruckus
all these sons of bitches in town and hell bent against us
who are they Virg
how about a quick drink
against the Earps
lets go down and disarm them
if you go down therell be a fight
their guns are legal inside the O.K. Corral but if they step into the street Ill have them surrender up their arms and arrest them
they wont hurt me Ill go down alone see if I cant disarm them
thats all I want to do
you all wait here
hello captain what do the vigilantes want
the cow-boys are making threats against you we can have men and arms ready ten in one minute
you can count on us
no thanks I wont bother them long as theyre only

getting horses to leave town
why I just come from there and theyre all down on Fremont Street now
why the cane Doc
where you going Wyatt
down the street for a fight
Ill go along
this is our fight no call for you to mix in
thats a hell of a thing to say to me
hold on you boys
whats that Virg
come with us Doc
amen brother
Wyatt those cow-boys are in the lot by the O.K. Corral back of Flys Boarding House which is Docs room to get a crack at him
all right but they aint giving up their arms this is a shootout and to the death

FOURTH STREET

By what light's coming through the overcast, in the frozen dirt, in hopes of peace, long shot, Wyatt Earp, and his blood, Virgil, Morgan, and his savior, Doc Holliday, walk up the street, by the American curse, by the inferno, and the silent iceman, by pages blowing into yesterday, go west on Fremont, by a whirl of yours truly and past due, ah the bad news, up at the lot, sidestep, out of the line of sight, to the wooden sidewalk.

Virg holds out the ten gauge, Doc hands him his cane, hides the shotgun under his long coat, as they go by all charges, all pleas, by the veins of silver, by the last words on the forsaken cross, Doc whistling quietly *Old times there are not forgotten*, by the meat market, by the assay office, by the boardinghouse, to the vacant lumberyard, back entrance to the O.K. Corral.

Johnny comes up, looking back, They won't give up their guns unless you do, What will you, I'm county sheriff, I won't allow this, they brush past him, For god's sake don't go in there or you'll be murdered, and Virg, I'm going to disarm them, switching the cane to his gun hand, his Army Colt revolver to his left hip, and Johnny, I have disarmed them, Wyatt shifting his long barrel six shooter into his overcoat pocket, Doc, the cold wind blowing his coat open over and over, showing the shotgun, Look out there on the flank, for an ambush, and somebody hollers, Here they come.

LUMBERYARD

in the empty yard black horse bay horse and back of them Tom McLaury hand on the rifle hanging from the saddle Frank McLaury in front Ike Clanton Billy Clanton hands down six yards away from Wyatt at the corner Doc in the street Morg at the sidewalk Virg into the yard

boys throw up your hands I want your guns

Frank thumbs back the hammer on his Colt Ike slips hand into his shirt Billy cocks Virg lifts his arms waving the cane

hold on I dont want that

the cow-boys backing up Wyatt going ahead and so shoot straighter Billy *any more horses to lose* draws across his body and fires Wyatt draws like lightning Billys no shot but Frank *ever follow us up this close well kill you* is dangerous he fires into his belly he staggers in the smoke fires back the horses screaming trying to bolt Tom *Ill fight you anywhere* fires over the top of them Virg switches the cane from hand to hand draws and fires at Tom at Billy Ike *Ill be ready for all of you* charges Wyatt slaps his arm his gun goes off Ike yelling

I am unarmed

Wyatt shoves him back

the fight has commenced get to shooting or get away

Ike runs toward the back of the boardinghouse Frank gutshot and moaning at the sidewalk fires back at Wyatt and his coat flaps Billy fires and Virg goes down clutching at his calf Morg fires hits Billy in the chest in the wrist in the belly he leans against the house slides down switches hands balances his pistol on his knee fires Morg falls

I am hit
holding his shoulder gets up trips on the water line trench Wyatt goes to shield him
stay down
Wyatt calm cracking off rounds fires at Tom whos shooting hits the horse in the withers and the horse runs Doc stalking Tom fires the shotgun into his armpit Tom staggers into the street Doc drops it draws fires twice at Billy Wyatt fires across the street at Frank bang from the alley but who or ricochet fires back Wyatt and Virg aim at Billy sitting down blood from his lips and fingers fire Frank has a horse by the reins fires at Morg and the horse breaks away he aims at Doc
I have you now you son of a bitch
youre a daisy if you do blaze away
Frank fires Doc looks at his hip
Im shot right through
Morg fires Doc fires at Frank hit in the head in the chest dying Doc runs at him
the son of a bitch has shot me and I mean to kill him
Tom dying at the telegraph pole on Third Wes picks up his gun Billy done for shoots wild into the air trying to reload Fly takes his pistol the hoisting works whistle blows Doc turns
what in helld you let Ike get away like that for Wyatt
he wouldnt jerk his gun

FREMONT STREET

What do I say, says the ghost bride, behind my veil, white smoke, to you, west cow-boy, at your last breath? Why did you come from the Lone Star plains, why did all your trails slope down, why did you drift into these badlands? To dance to the fiddle of crime, against the gospel, against possession, against blood? To live outside the law of skin, and shoot them down who consecrate it? To be condemned to this prison of light? Why didn't you claim me with a territorial kiss? Why was there no shivaree, of bells and banging? Why didn't you pioneer into me? For you, there is no woman, only the October wind, and disgrace, staining the dust of the street, no house, only the pine box under the hill, no sunrise girl, no boy under the setting moon, only the lies on your headstone, no days to come, only these last questions. And your mortal soul? It went nowhere, it bubbled out of your lips and rose, not to heaven, not to the stars, not to the steeple, only as high as your sombrero when you were standing, where it fizzled and was gone. I have nothing. Like you, I am nothing.

4

FREMONT STREET

out of the sheriffs office
Wyatt I'm arresting you
for what
for murder
any officer that was on the square Id let him not you
and the theater manager
dont be in a hurry to arrest this man he done right in killing them the people will uphold him
we done right we had to do it and you threw us Johnny
what do you mean
you told us they was disarmed you lied to throw us get us murdered
youre under arrest
not today not tomorrow Ill be in town

PRAYER FOR THE DEAD

Brass band
in the lead of the procession:
dead march:
hearse:
body in casket with silver:
name age birthplace date of death:
hearse:
bodies in caskets:
in a wagon, brothers:
hundreds, walking,
mourning: or rid of them:
carriages buckboards stagecoach men on horses:
witnesses in the dust
on the long trail up to Boot Hill.

SIXTH STREET

Doc with his hand on his wound
back in this hole goddamn it I cant keep out of it
this time with bail revoked
if this is to be my roost I swear if Tombstone cant
afford it Ill take up a collection for an actual jail
Wyatt looking out on the street as the light fails
least we got vigilantes watching out for assassina-
tion
ah my hip how is it everyone in that shoot up was
shot but you
I dont know how I go where the bullets aint
and this you what picked up in your old gunfights
I aint been in a gunfight before
well bless my soul
I aint never shot a man before
those outlaws had it coming it was a luminous
stand
it dont make it easy Doc
ah deacon your wounds inside
think the grand jury will take up the charge
well theyve assembled all of the best surviving
liars as witnesses Billy Allen Johnny Behan Kid
Claiborne Wes Fuller
and who is this other McLaury brother
hes in from Texas to lawyer for the prosecution
said I think we can hang them
what theyre saying is absurd that they were un-
armed with their hands up and that you shot first
with a pistol how could you when youre holding
a shotgun
the beauty of lying is anything is possible
yeah but Ike Clantons stories all fly apart and
only weaken their case
in the hands of the judge

I testify tomorrow
that what you been writing
yes by statute I can testify from a document with-
out cross if nothing else before were executed they
can hear the gods truth

the difficulty which resulted in the death of Billy Clanton and Frank and Tom McLaury originated last spring a little over a year ago I followed Frank and Tom McLaury and two other parties who had stolen six government mules from Camp Rucker myself Virg and Morg Earp and Marshal Williams Captain Hurst and four soldiers we traced those mules to McLaurys ranch also found the branding iron D8 and after quite a while the mules were found with the same brand they tried to pick a fuss out of me down there and told me if I ever followed them up again as close as I did they would kill me Captain Hurst came to us boys and told us he had made this compromise by so doing he would get his mules back we insisted on following them up Hurst prevailed on us to go back to Tombstone and so we came back they would not give up the mules to him after we went saying that they only wanted to get us away that they could stand the soldiers off Captain Hurst cautioned me and my brothers Virgil and Morgan to look out for those men that they had made some hard threats against our lives

shortly after the time Bud Philpott was killed by the men who tried to rob the Benson stage as a detective I helped trace the matter up and I was satisfied that three men named Bill Leonard Harry the Kid and Slim Jim Crane were in that robbery I knew that they were friends and associates of the Clantons and McLaurys and often stopped at their ranches it was generally understood among officers and those who have information about criminals that Ike Clanton was a sort of chief among the cow-boys that the Clantons and McLaurys were cattle thieves and generally in on the secret of the stage robbery and that the Clanton and McLaury ranches were meeting places and places of shelter for the gang I was satisfied that Frank and Tom McLaury killed and robbed Mexicans in the Skeleton Canyon two or three months ago and I naturally kept my eyes open I did not intend that any of the band should get the drop on me . . .

I believed then and believe now from the acts I have stated and the threats I have related and other threats communicated to me by different persons as having been made by Tom McLaury Frank McLaury and Ike Clanton that these men last named had formed a conspiracy to murder my brothers Morgan and Virgil and Doc Holliday and myself I believe I would have been legally and morally justified in shooting any of them on sight but I did not do so nor attempt to do so I sought no advantage when I went as deputy marshal to help disarm them and arrest them I went as part of my duty and under the direction of my brother the marshal I did not intend to fight unless it became necessary in self defense and in the performance of official duty when Billy Clanton and Frank McLaury drew their pistols I knew it was a fight for life and I drew and fired in defense of my own life and the lives of my brothers and Doc Holliday

JUDGE'S OFFICE

(reading)

The Court: Considering all the testimony together I am of the opinion that the weight of evidence sustains and corroborates the testimony of Wyatt and Virgil Earp that their demand for surrender was met by William Clanton and Frank McLaury drawing, or making motions to draw, their pistols. Upon this hypothesis my duty is clear. The defendants were officers charged with the duty of arresting and disarming brave and determined men who were experts in the use of firearms, as quick as thought and certain as death, and who had previously declared their intention not to be arrested or disarmed.

In coming to this conclusion I give great weight to several particular circumstances connected with the affray. It is claimed by the prosecution that the deceased were shot while holding up their hands in obedience to the demand of the chief of police, and on the other hand the defense claims that William Clanton and Frank McLaury at once drew their pistols and began firing simultaneously with the defendants. William Clanton was wounded on the wrist of the right hand on the first fire and thereafter used his pistol with his left. This wound is such as could not have been received with his hands thrown up, and the wound received by Thomas McLaury was such as could not have been received with his hands on his coat lapels. These circumstances, being indubitably facts, throw great doubt on the correctness of statements of witnesses to the contrary.

The testimony of Isaac Clanton that this tragedy was the result of a scheme on the part of the Earps to assassinate him, and thereby bury in oblivion the confessions the Earps had made to him about piping away the shipment of coin by Wells, Fargo & Co., falls short of a sound theory because of the great fact, most prominent in the matter, to wit, that Isaac Clanton was not injured at all, and could have been killed first and easiest. If it was the object of the attack to kill him he would have been the first to fall, but as it was, he was known or believed to be unarmed, and was suffered, so Wyatt Earp testifies, to go away and was not harmed.

In view of the past history of the county and the generally believed existence at this time of desperate, reckless and lawless men in our midst, banded together for mutual support, and living by felonious and predatory pursuits, regarding neither lives nor property in their career, and at this time for men to parade the streets armed with repeating rifles and six-shooters and demand that the chief of police of the city and his assistants should be disarmed is a proposition both monstrous and startling. This was said by one of the deceased only a few minutes before the arrival of the Earps.

Another fact that rises up preeminent in the consideration of this sad affair is the leading fact that the deceased from the very first inception of the encounter were standing their ground and fighting back, giving and taking death with unflinching bravery. It does not appear to have been a wanton slaughter of unresisting and unarmed innocents, who were yielding graceful submission to the officers of the law, or surrendering to or fleeing from their assailants, but armed and defiant men, accepting the wager of battle and succumbing only in death.

I cannot resist the conclusion that the defendants were fully justified in committing these homicides, that it was a necessary act done in the discharge of official duty.

COSMOPOLITAN HOTEL

who was the woman in a veil
who knocked last night
I hear she left without a word
it was a man Sadie
assassin
looking for me or my brothers
the Epitaph says
judge attorney agent mayor
the rumors are
and Doc all marked for death
they more than talk
look out this window
at what the Grand
you see that shutter
with one slat open
its for a rifle
who is in there
Curley Bill Johnny Ringo
across from your rooms
Ike Clanton Pony Deal
they wont shoot the sheriff
Im not running
not against Johnny
that sheet the Nuggets lies
was talking to Big Nose Kate
what does she say
Ringo told her go back to Globe
what
theyre going to gun down Doc
who is
the Clantons
it never ends
at Flys Boarding House
Im in a prospect hole

why honey
killing them boys
it was them or you
I think of him
of him
the only begotten
ah the savior
this catechism
in the gospel
who perishes
they that take the sword
who is blessed
the peacemaker
who do you love
your enemies
his hand his hand
but you know that
is open
they drove a nail
to kill to live
if we have to
what kind of life
its life
heroes
our saviors
walking in blood
ah love
lets get out of here
we can go out
where to
the Bird Cage Theatre opened
dont Dutch Annie have
yeah cribs in there

why go
sawbuck for a soiled dove
dont need any sweetheart
and snake water
never touch it
Little Egypt is dancing
whos she
she does the belly dance
she does
bare breasts
I dont know
Docs dealing faro
lets go

FIFTH STREET

Xmas, sagebrush trees strung with cranberries, hung with candles, and three days after, late night, Virg comes out of the Oriental, on the way to the hotel, watching Frank Stilwell go into the old Palace Saloon, burned out, and his arm shatters, bang, double barrel shotgun, bang, bang and his back's on fire, as he goes down, the gunmen run down Fifth, Head them off, past the ice house, the Combination shaft, down Toughnut, below the hoisting works, into the Gulch, riding out toward Charleston. He hunches into the Oriental looking for Wyatt, till he slops blood at his brother's feet; this miner says, Sorry for you, Virg, and he, It's hell, ain't it. When the sawbones show, Wyatt crosses the street, and out of the ashes by the window, he picks up Ike Clanton's hat.

WESTERN UNION TELEGRAPH COMPANY

Dated Tombstone December 29 1881
Received at 12 PM
To US Marshal Crawley Dake Phoenix

Virgil shot last night assassins in hiding wounds mortal local authorities doing nothing federal troops not coming to Cochise County wire me appointment power deputies lives here under threat

Wyatt Earp

ALLEN STREET

Johnny Ringos hand on his gun Doc Hollidays inside his vest
you been shooting your mouth off about me Holliday
I have and I repeat it now Im sorry to see a first class cattle thief like yourself fall in with assassins
youre going to publicly take back all youve said
what I said goes
youre going to meet your shadow
lets move into the street so no one else will be hurt
officer grabs Ringo from behind
turn him loose Flynn Ringo you can start shooting
Wyatt tugs on his arm
quit this foolishness
nodding at the window in the Grand Hotel with a rifle muzzle pulling back in
one move and he wouldve dropped you

for the love of god Doc I cant let you buck out in smoke and dont think I dont know why youre aiming for him it aint cause he got away with that stage robbery by threatening the driver its cause hes been galling Big Nose Kate look I have federal money to go hunt down the men who shot Virg you hear what he said Never mind Allie I got one arm left to hug you I want you in my posse seven men warrants for Ike and Fin Clanton and Pony Deal and you know what the judge said handing them over Youll never clean up this crowd that way Youd best leave your prisoners in the mesquite where alibis dont matter were searching Charleston and the hills outside and down the river in the back country when we get close theyll think its only mail theft and give themselves up but bang its attempted murder are you with me much obliged

TOMBSTONE, FEBRUARY 1, 1882

Major C. P. Dake, United States Marshal
Grand Hotel
Tombstone

Dear Sir,

Acting in our official role as Deputy U.S. Marshals in this Territory, we have tried, always, without flinching, to deliver on the duties given in trust to us. They've been a hard go, dangerous, and had to be done in a settlement where sprees and shootouts could break out anytime. And why, to cross, in contempt, our carrying out the writs and warrants of the court, handed down to haul outlaws to justice. We are deeply obliged to many for their steady help in reining in crime, and for their faith that what we do is honest. But though we reckon as best we can, and do our damnedest at what we've been asked, it doesn't matter. Stage holdups go on, the cow-boys have alibis, there's a death list, and talk of a raid on us. Mexico may go to war to stop their rustling, and so they're forced to steal in our county. Wells, Fargo & Co. are threatening to close. In the election, the cow-boys won out. They have the mayor and the sheriff in their pocket. Their yellow journal prints bad words about us, over and over, warping and darkening what we've done, till the citizens don't know what to believe. And that leads us to this. To show them that we're true, and our intent's to do them good, without thought for our own gain or how we're advanced, it's our duty to put our resignations as Deputy U.S. Marshals in your hands, and turn in our stars. We're grateful that we've been so long in your favor, and that you're sure of our integrity. We know you may not accept this offer, and till you've appointed the men who'll replace us, we'll go on doing what you give us to do.

Very respectfully yours,
Virgil W. Earp
Wyatt S. Earp

FREMONT STREET

I have a warrant
read it Johnny
to any sheriff constable marshal or policeman in the Territory of Arizona greetings you are commanded to arrest Wyatt Earp Morgan Earp Virgil Earp and J. H. Holliday and bring them forthwith before me at my office on Main Street in the Village of Contention in the County of Cochise Territory of Arizona J. B. Smith Justice of the Peace
the charges have already been rejected by judge and jury
not my concern
Ike has no new evidence
you men are under arrest
I can smell this
give me your guns and get in the buckboard
so we can be ambushed out on Contention Road
go to hell
who are
my army twelve men with revolvers and rifles in the buggy with a Winchester is my lawyer
lets go
you ride ahead

5

ATTORNEY'S OFFICE

out the window no stars
they were after us last night
think so
you represent them
just business
you know anything
nothing
get an answer from Ike
no truce
think were in danger
youre liable to get it any time
I didnt see nobody
I think
different in town
I see strangers here
who is it
I think are after you
who
Ringo asked me to tell you
tell me
if any fight happened hes clear
that so
everybodys on their own
whos that below
Stilwell I better go
the window rattling

CAMPBELL AND HATCH'S SALOON

in rain and wind
one game
no lets go back
what for
he saw armed men
you walked around
yes Morg
see anyone
Apache Hank
no threat
Indian Charlie
come on
you like the show
well Stolen Kisses
yeah hard not to
Sadie go back
yeah to Frisco
Lou wrote
California girls
out of danger
hey theres Big Tip
rack em up Wyatt
you love sixty-one
aint that the truth
go on and break
okay Im solids
you following up
on what
well on the thief
what thief
who stole the kisses
ah hah
the wall is dust

over Wyatt's head
what the
Morg folds over
two shots
glass door shattered
from the alley
Morg slides down
Wyatt hauls on him
dont boys I cant stand it
that bad
I played my last game
hound at the door howling
Morg whispering
ear to his brother's lips
guess you were right Wyatt
on what
the heaven after
I remember
I cant see a damn thing
ah Morg
you know who done it
I do
wish I could get em
Ill get em for you
all I ask but Wyatt
yeah Morg
be so careful
wind blowing in through the holes in the back
door

BENSON ROAD

At noon, on Sunday, his birthday, in the merciless light, the fire bell ringing dust to dust, Wyatt Earp follows his brother's slow funeral, from the hotel, with the departed in a spring wagon, to the iron station, and the train to haul him to his woman to bury.

He heads back on the old stage road, so many times, with the ruts holding out against the sagebrush, and the mesquite threatening in the dusk, and he curls over the thorn of his loss, keeping back any tears, all the way into Tombstone, to the one saloon.

senor mi amigo you have always been welcoming when I cross the street and you are U.S. Marshal and your brother was shot I have to tell you if Spence kills me dios de mi vida last Saturday I was at home and my husband was gone two days in Charleston and he comes home at noon comes in with two men Freeze I dont know the others name they had rifles he sent a man to look after los caballos then they go into the front room and talk to Stilwell then Stilwell goes out and Spence to bed and this is all that night Spence gets up at nine o'clock Sunday Freeze was sleeping there the other man goes home on Friday and stays there all day goes out Friday night but comes back in a little while to sleep Saturday hes out all day till midnight and Spence comes in Indian Charlie is with Stilwell he has a pistol and a carbine he goes out Saturday morning with Stilwell and comes back with him at midnight both of them armed with pistols and carbines when they come back to the house Saturday night all their talk Spence and Stilwell and los otros hombres is in low voices like they are telling a secret when they come in I get out of bed to receive them and I see theyre excited why I dont know Stilwell comes into the house and after an hour Spence and the others Stilwell gives me a message from Spence Ill be up from Charleston that night Saturday I was told at two o'clock think Spence left last night for Sonora dont know for sure he went Sunday morning Spence says get breakfast it was about six o'clock which I did but before that we had a fight and he hit me and mi madre Francisca and he says hell shoot me and my mother says hell have to shoot her too he says Marietta if you say one word about anything you know Ill kill you Im going to Sonora and Ill leave your dead body behind me Spence didnt say so but yo se el lo mato I know one of them killed Morg I think they did it because he comes to the house all shaking and the others who come in with him teeth chattering when he comes in I ask you want some sopa and he says I do not myself and mi madre we hear the shots and it was a little while after Stilwell and Charlie come in and a half hour after Spence and the others I think Spence and the others they might have come in the night they left their horses outside of town and after the shooting went and got them I judge theyve been doing wrong because theyre white and shaking when they come in Spence and the others for days always leave home in the middle of the day and come back in the middle of the night but they never come back in the shape they were in that night and the next morning after hearing that Morg died I see that Stilwell and the others did this deed I have not seen Charlie since that night dont know where he is last week my mother and I were standing on the veranda talking with Spence and Charlie and Morg passes by and Spence nudges Charlie and says thats him thats him and Charlie runs down the street so he can get ahead of him and get a look at him

SOUTHERN PACIFIC

the desert going dark
wish I could go after them Wyatt
well you aint
I know I aint mended
I cant look after you Virg and them
you got federal warrants
first thing
your posse
Doc Holliday Texas Jack
good boys
Scar Face brother Warren
yeah yeah
Turkey Creek Johnson
out of Deadwood
from the two against one gunfight
by the graveyard road
you go home to mama and daddy
whyre we stopping
dont know still east of the Tucson station
you Wyatt Earp
yes
Im Deputy U.S. Marshal Evans
what is it
this is a warning
you caught your breath
Frank Stilwell Ike Clanton
I know them
Pete Spence and a breed I dont know
Indian Charlie
in town watching the trains for you
his brother in the lighted window
get down Virg and you Allie
Tucson Station
goodbye Virg

Ill be seeing you
Ill be seeing you soon
take care
Wyatt leans out of the vestibule

TUCSON STATION

Wyatt Earp sees them in a flatcar on the next track, on their bellies. He slips out of the train, back way, to the platform, and there's the glow of the gaslight on the barrels of their guns. His shotgun on his arm, he walks over to them, and they drop theirs and run. He chases Stilwell, who crosses the tracks, at last stands, won't draw, shaking, and wrestles for Wyatt's shotgun, Wyatt gets the muzzle over his heart, Stilwell yelling, Morg! Morg! and Wyatt, You see a ghost? and fires. You are a ghost. He lights out after Ike, when a train pulls out between them, and he loses him. He runs up to the window, It's all right, Virg: one for Morg! and holds up a finger. He walks back to Stilwell's body. Doc is shooting it, in the armpit, in the leg, in the hand.

COSMOPOLITAN HOTEL

whos there
the colonel
come on in
who are all these
my posse
whats going on
the telegraph operator woke me saying theres a
message for Johnny from Tucson that Doc and I
are accused of murder for shooting Stilwell
was it a warrant from the county sheriff
thats what I said and no it was Ike Clanton saying
hed sworn out that charge
and the operator
was warning me I said you deliver it not yet can
you hold off long as you say one hour will do tell
my lawyer
I advise you to surrender to Johnny
not going to
you can clear yourself easy
one Id lose days chasing the assassins two if Im
disarmed Ill be shot three he dont have the right
or the authority to arrest me
what about
I have a mission and Johnny aint going to get in
the way
what about the county sheriff
tell him Ill surrender any time
all right
and the document making over all my property
from soda to hock to my daddy
sign here
Turkey Creek Texas Jack
yeah Wyatt
pack up the camp supplies saddle the horses whos

there
the vigilante
come on in
Johnnys in the lobby with a deputy and two in the street
colonel you better wait here till this is over
hell no I want to see this
Wyatt buckles on his six gun his Wells Fargo shotgun on his arm
Ill go down first Doc you come last
at the top of the stairs
remember boys no gunplay
and they walk down
this aint none of my affair Wyatt
the deputy
but the sheriffs going to arrest you and he thought we could avoid some trouble if I talked to you first
Wyatt looking at Johnny
avoid some trouble tell that coward I got a double eagle for him if hell only try to arrest me
Johnny goes out to his deputies Wyatt pays the hotel bill
come on boys
Johnny turns to him
Wyatt I want to see you
you cant see me youre going to see me once too often
Wyatt swings into his saddle as his posse heads out sun going down he lights a cigar wheels and rides down Allen Street to the hills south

SOUTH PASS

hands down your alias Indian Charlie
si the vaqueros call me that
cause youre a breed well Florentino birth dont matter what matters is how big a hole after your death
in the yellow grass bone trees and the Dragoons warping into the sky
you can walk though youre shot
si senor
around the shoulder out of sight of the waterhole
I had Scar Face hit you in the thigh not kill you so we could jaw a little
si senor I dont steal horse
I have a warrant for you on a murder count and the mid air dance you out with it we can go easy
I no confess nothing
I was talking to these boys to let you try to go on the dodge when you seen me you did up that slope you going belly through the brush thats your confession
in a sweat drags off his bandanna
they was going one two times they was going to ambush Holliday
who was
Ike Clanton Frank Stilwell they ambush Virgil and Ringo in on it
Ike and Frank doing the shooting
si they ambush you and Morgan that night Curley Bill missing you from the alley and Frank shooting Morgan through the glass
in the back like always any of you with sand enough to face us and you
I was lookout on Allen Street and Ringo with the horses on Fremont and another man I dont know

walked in with the
hes lying
I know Doc hes covering for Apache Hank that it
Frank left his cut horse in the arroyo at the edge of Tombstone we finish off the Earp brothers and theres no reason to run
his getaway
I had to ride him to Pattersons ranch I know you smoked him thats all I know
thisll be good testimony you can go with Turkey Creek hold on
que senor
my brothers and I we ever hurt you
no senor
why help kill Morgan
it was my amigos Curley Bill give me 25 silver dollars
25
opening his long duster
thats a number Ive got another number for you 3
you can draw when you like I wont till 3
no senor
dropping his bandanna
uno
bleak morning the cicadas chirring
dos

UNANSWERED PRAYER

Skin and bones Jesus,
out fishing for men in unredeemed Missouri,
in the tallgrass, sundown,
so north, where my woman lies, unrisen,
and where I saw
in the skies license, in the rains mercy,
I count this man's black wounds,
the thigh, by my order,
the gut, by me,
the back, the temple, by my companion,
blood everywhere,
cross me
with only a crack of the light of justice
in this country, this territory, this fucking mesa.

IRON SPRINGS

Agents in Charleston say that Curley Bill is in the Barbacomari wilderness. On a vendetta ride Wyatt Earp racks after him, from the San Pedro River, long dry trail north, to the Whetstone Mountains, to get one thousand dollars for his posse at the waterhole at Iron Springs. At the trail forks, no sign of travel, for days. He has his brother wait for the money, rides up a skinny canyon in the infernal sun, and still no sign, lets down his vigilance, unbuttons his coat, loosens his gunbelt. He's carrying his Colt single-action .45 with a long barrel and a walnut handle, in the saddle boot, a Winchester .44-40, looped to the saddle horn, a cartridge belt, in a pommel strap, a 12-gauge Remington sawed off shotgun.

Down slope, past a rock shoulder, across a sand flat, hidden, back of a cut bank and hollow, is Iron Springs, beyond, an abandoned shack, and a grove of cottonwoods. His horse is quickening at the smell of water. It's wrong, he dismounts, slides out his shotgun, walks on, no sound. At the edge of the bluff, he can see down in the hollow, man lifting his shotgun, man cutting for the woods. Scar Face yells, Curley Bill! and rides the other way, bullets coming, Texas Jack's horse goes down on his leg, the posse going for cover in a cloud.

His horse spooking, and he throws the bridle over his arm, too wild, he can't get on. If my time's come, he's going with me. At the gully, he sees Curley Bill squint his left eye and sight with his right along his shotgun, he *I done nothing* fires,

Wyatt's long coat flares. He missed me, I can't miss him. He fires, one barrel, the other, into the gut, cutting him in half, and the cow-boy yells in agony with his last breath.

He sees the gold-mount ivory-handle six guns that Curley Bill had stolen in that stage holdup. Pony Deal, Rattlesnake Bill, and all the rest, are running, he has warrants for all of them, they shoot wild into his coat. I should have saved the other barrel, cut holes in them. His horse rearing, he can't get his rifle, his gunbelt's slipped, he reaches down the back of his leg for his Special. Where in hell is the posse? riding away. He turns and fires into the band of angels, gets yells, he smells sulfur, as a bullet hits the saddle horn.

He's on his horse, and fires toward the hill of the skull, no answer, slides out his rifle, turns back to Texas Jack, who's hauling his saddle, shotgun, boot and all, away from his dead horse, Doc giving a hand. Wyatt fires twice into the row of crosses, shots coming back, and his leg is numb, only hit the bootheel.

WHETSTONE MOUNTAINS

Wyatt you must be all shot to pieces
no Doc
whats all this
only the skirts of my coat
miracle nobody hit
well you was riding away
not cold-footed only in cover
I couldnt see nowhere to go
you walk right in he had the deadwood on you
I made a promise
theyre on the run lets go finish them
ah no Ive had enough
saying you wont pursue
the angels the angels
the what
want war go on and get your fill
but its the goddamn cow-boys
without their leader theyll unravel
yeah but theres still Johnny Ringo
what will happen is who you are
I see hes always been down bound
hell shoot himself in the temple mystery why
and Ike Clanton goes on getting indicted
hell meet a lawman at last who wont spare him
and Johnny Behan the guardian of dishonor
hell go on cheating with money itll catch up
wasnt there money for us at Iron Springs
yeah and the gunfight come between
youre in for the thousand dollars on Curley Bills head
hell no I done this for my brother
well you shot up his outlaws the sheriffs coming
I reckon we can head up to the Sierra Bonita
thats General Hookers spread we can rest our

horses
theres a bluff north where we can make a stand
youre right the sheriffs all show and wont charge
head on out to Colorado
I prophesy your San Francisco love
if I have any future its with her
cant follow you into that weather its adios
but not tonight old friend
thats music to me
know what I want
no what
a shot of whiskey

SULPHUR SPRINGS VALLEY

Wyatt Earp, followed by his posse, following nobody, rides north into the desolate playa, no life, not even vultures, for miles across the dead lake, to the edge and saltgrass, in the distance between desire and consummation, on a chance horse, its hooves lifting alkali dust.

He takes up the old trail, into the back country, ah god, that blood, at morning, red, unknown, the sighs, the blood, downpouring: and it's no good, can't dream, with a dead soul. What's the difference? Murder, everywhere on this ball, here, or across the line, in the high plains.

Last light, last prayer, on the Chiricahuas, and the light going, and meaning, as the territory pitches into the dark, and he rides on, toward the ghost hills.

Ballad of Mattie

SOURCES

1

Testimony for the Defense—Statement by Wyatt Earp. 1881, in Stephens and Martin
How Wyatt Earp Routed a Gang of Arizona Outlaws. Wyatt Earp Tells Tales of the Shotgun-Messenger Service. Wyatt Earp's Tribute to Bat Masterson the Hero of 'Dobe Wells. 1896, in Stephens
Wyatt Earp. John Flood, 1926
Tombstone: An Iliad of the Southwest. Chapter II-XV. Walter Burns, 1927
Wyatt Earp: Frontier Marshal. Stuart Lake, 1931

2

Dodge City. Michael Curtiz, director; Robert Buckner, writer, 1939
Frontier Marshal. All Duan, director; Sam Hellman, writer, 1939
Tombstone. William McGann, director; Albert LeVino, Edward Paramore, writers, 1942
My Darling Clementine. John Ford, director; Samuel Engel, Winston Miller, writers, 1946
Wichita. Jacques Tourneur, director; Daniel Ullman, writer, 1955
Gunfight at the O.K. Corral. John Sturges, director; Leon Uris, writer, 1957
The Life and Legend of Wyatt Earp. 15 historical episodes. Lewis Foster, Frank McDonald, Roy Rowland, Paul Landres, directors; Frederick Brennan, writer, 1955-61
Hour of the Gun. John Sturges, director; Edward Anhalt, writer, 1967
Tombstone. George Cosmatos, director; Kevin Jarre, writer, 1993
The American Experience. Wyatt Earp. Rob Rapley, producer, 2010

3

Wyatt Earp Speaks. Edited by John Stephens, 1998
Tombstone's Epitaph. Douglas Martin, 1951 (autographed by the author and a relative of Holliday)
Inventing Wyatt Earp: His Life and Many Legends. Allen Barra, 1998
True West. Wyatt Earp: Without a Scratch. Bob Bell, 2001
The Illustrated Life & Times of Wyatt Earp. Bob Bell, 2008
Wyatt Earp. Philip Ketchum, 1956
Gunfight at the O.K. Corral. Nelson Nye, 1960
Wild, Wooly & Wicked: The History of Kansas Cow Towns and the Texas Cattle Trade. Harry Drago, 1960
A Treasury of Western Folklore. B. A. Botkin, 1975
Western Words: A Dictionary of the Old West. Ramon Adams, 1981
My Darling Clementine: John Ford, Director. Edited by Robert Lyons, 1984
Explore America: Wild Kingdoms. Edited by Alfred Le Maitre, Elizabeth Leavis, 1996
Wyatt Earp: The Life Behind the Legend. Casey Tefertiller, 1997
Everyday Life in the Wild West. Candy Moulton, 1999
The Six-Gun Mystique Sequel. John Cawetti, 1999
Tombstone's Treasure: Silver Mines and Golden Saloons. Sherry Monahan, 2007
www.LegendsofAmerica.com, 2012

4

Revelation: 8. John of Patmos, 96
Lucrece. William Shakespeare, 1594
74, in Shakespeares Sonnets. William Shakespeare, 1609
The Design of Rimbaud's Poetry. John Houston, 1963
The Artistry of Shakespeare's Prose. Brian Vickers, 1968
Shakespeare's Use of Rhetoric, in A New Companion to Shakespeare Studies. Brian Vickers, 1971

The Lost Garden: A View of Shakespeare's English and Roman History Plays. John Wilders, 1978
Language in Literature. Roman Jakobson, 1987
The Development of Shakespeare's Rhetoric: A Study of Nine Plays. Stefan Keller, 2009

ABOUT THE AUTHOR

Larry Beckett's poetry ranges from songs, like the modern standard "Song to the Siren," to blank sonnets, *Songs and Sonnets*, published by Rainy Day Women Press, to the epic *American Cycle:* out of which come *Paul Bunyan*, from Smokestack Books, *Amelia Earhart*, from Finishing Line Press, and this volume. *Beat Poetry* is a study of the poets and poetry of the fifties San Francisco renaissance.

ABOUT THE COVER

A daguerreotype is a photograph taken using a lengthy process that involved polishing a sheet of silver-plated copper to a mirror finish. The plate was exposed to iodine fumes to sensitize the silver, exposed in the camera, then exposed to mercury fumes to develop the image. A rinse in a saltwater solution stabilized the photo.

The plate was the photo; no duplicates could be made. In that sense it was like today's Polaroid images, but with much more work and with exposure to dangerous chemicals. This image of Wyatt Earp would have been taken during the waning days of the daguerreotype, when he was in his early twenties.

I used modern digital techniques, so we can view his face clearly without taking away the feel of the original. I left the patina very much as it would have been when first taken.

—Laura Fletcher

Laura Fletcher is a fine art and natural-light portrait photographer. She has been in and out of the dark since she was born. Her mother, who grew up using box cameras, taught her photography from both sides of the camera. Laura thinks life is worth treasuring, and she does that through photography.

COLOPHON

The edition you are holding is the First Edition of this publication.

The signature on the cover is Wyatt Earp's actual signature, created into a font by Leah Angstman. The distressed font is Nashville, created by Disturbed Type to emulate *Wanted* posters of the Wild West. The numbers are set in Duality, created by Typodermic Fonts. The ampersand on the back cover is set in 1550, created by Frédéric Michaud. All other text is set in Marion, created by Ray Larabie, based on vintage press plates. The Alternating Current Press logo is set in Portmanteau, created by JLH Fonts. All fonts used with permission; all rights reserved.

Front cover daguerreotype restored by Laura Fletcher. Cover designed by Leah Angstman.

The Alternating Current lightbulb logo was created by Leah Angstman, ©2013, 2020 Alternating Current. Larry Beckett's photo was taken by Laura Fletcher, ©2020. All material used with permission; all rights reserved.

OTHER WORKS FROM
ALTERNATING CURRENT PRESS

All of these books (and more) are available at Alternating Current's website: press.alternatingcurrentarts.com.

Download a free professional live recording of the author reading this longform poem

SCAN ME

Printed in Great Britain
by Amazon

33744509R00081